Dinosaurs and the Age of Reptiles

Christopher Lampton

DINOSAURS AND THE AGE OF REPTILES

A GROLIER COMPANY

FRANKLIN WATTS
NEW YORK | LONDON | TORONTO | SYDNEY | 1983
A FIRST BOOK

Cover photograph courtesy of
the National Museum of Natural History,
Smithsonian Institution.

Photographs courtesy of
The American Museum of Natural History:
pp. 7 (both), 8, 12, 15, 16, 66, 74–75;
The Field Museum of Natural History, Chicago:
pp. 29, 39, 76;
© The Field Museum of Natural History,
paintings by Charles R. Knight:
pp. 30–31, 34, 37, 40–41,
48–49, 50, 53, 55, 62–63;
National Museum of Natural History,
Smithsonian Institution:
pp. 54, 59.

Diagram courtesy of Vantage Art, Inc.

Library of Congress Cataloging in Publication Data

Lampton, Christopher.
Dinosaurs and the age of reptiles.

(A First book)
Bibliography: p.
Includes index.
Summary: Describes the origin of dinosaurs,
their characteristics, and their eventual
disappearance. Also discusses the discovery
and investigation of dinosaur fossils and
other kinds of reptiles that lived during
the age of dinosaurs.
1. Dinosaurs—Juvenile literature.
2. Reptiles, Fossil—Juvenile literature.
[1. Dinosaurs. 2. Reptiles, Fossil] I. Title.
QE862.D5L425 1983 567.9'1 82-16087
ISBN 0-531-04526-9

Printed in the United States of America
5 4 3

Contents

Dinosaurs and the Age of Reptiles

Dinosaur

NAME	SUBORDER	FAMILY
Allosaurus	Theropod	Megalosaur
Anatosaurus	Ornithopod	Hadrosaur
Ankylosaurus	Ankylosaur	Nodosaur
Apatosaurus (aka Brontosaurus)	Sauropod	Brachiosaur
Brachiosaurus	Sauropod	Brachiosaur
Camptosaurus	Ornithopod	Iguanodont
Ceolophysis	Theropod	Hallopod
Compsognathus	Theropod	Coeluridae
Diplodocus	Sauropod	Titanosaur
Gorgosaurus	Theropod	Tyrannosaur
Hadrosaurus	Ornithopod	Hadrosaur
Hypsilophodon	Ornithopod	Hypsilophodont
Iguanodon	Ornithopod	Iguanodont
Megalosaurus	Theropod	Megalosaur
Monoclonius	Ceratopsian	Ceratopsidae
Plateosaurus	Theropod	Plateosaur
Psittacosaurus	Ceratopsian	Psittacosaur
Stegosaurus	Stegosaur	Stegosauridae
Triceratops	Ceratopsian	Ceratopsidae
Tyrannosaurus	Theropod	Tyrannosaur

Chart

DIET	PERIOD	COMMENTS
Carnivore	Mid & Lower Jurassic	Greatest Jurassic predator
Herbivore	Upper Cretaceous	Duck-billed dinosaur
Herbivore	Upper Cretaceous	Club-like tail
Herbivore	Mid & Upper Jurassic	Best known dinosaur
Herbivore	Mid & Upper Jurassic	Largest animal ever
Herbivore	Mid & Lower Jurassic	Ancestor of thecodonts
Herbivore	Upper Triassic	Small, early dinosaur
Herbivore	Upper Jurassic	Smallest known dinosaur
Herbivore	Mid & Upper Jurassic	Longest known dinosaur
Carnivore	Upper Cretaceous	Giant predator
Herbivore	Upper Cretaceous	Duck-billed dinosaur
Herbivore	Late Cretaceous	First ornithischian
Herbivore	Late Cretaceous	First dinosaur fossil identified
Carnivore	Jurassic	First dinosaur named
Herbivore	Upper Cretaceous	Giant horned dinosaur
Herbivore	Upper Triassic	Largest Triassic reptile
Herbivore	Late Cretaceous	Parrot-beaked dinosaur
Herbivore	Upper Jurassic	Armored dinosaur
Herbivore	Upper Cretaceous	Largest ceratopsian
Carnivore	Upper Cretaceous	Largest theropod

(1) The World of Reptiles

The world of 150 million years ago was different in a great many ways from the world we live in today. If you saw a map of the world as it looked then, you might not even recognize it as your own.

All the familiar continents—including North and South America, Asia, Europe, and Australia—were linked together into two giant supercontinents. Today, we refer to these ancient supercontinents as Gondwanaland (in the south) and Laurasia (in the north). Between these continents lay a mighty body of water called the Tethys. Eventually, these supercontinents broke up and drifted apart to form the modern continents. (In fact, the modern continents are still drifting. Europe and America are moving away from one another at a rate of a couple of inches a year, for example.)

The vegetation of this ancient world was not much like that of today's, either. There were no flowering plants, for instance, but there were giant ferns and mosses that grew as big as modern trees.

The strangest thing about this bygone earth, however, concerned the animals that lived on it. Today, most of the large animals that live on the earth are mammals. One of the ways that you can recognize mammals is that they have hair on their bodies. Human beings are mammals. Dogs and cats are mammals. Monkeys and gorillas are mammals. Elephants are mammals. Even whales and dolphins, though they live in the ocean, are mammals.

In the world of 150 million years ago, however, the only mammals were small creatures that lived in holes in the ground and in trees. None was larger than a cat. Most were as small as mice. In those days, the earth was populated by reptiles.

Today, most reptiles are small creatures (with some notable exceptions, such as crocodiles, which can grow up to 30 feet, or 12 meters, long). When we think of reptiles we tend to think of animals such as snakes and turtles. The ancestors of modern snakes and turtles were alive in this world of 150 million years ago. So were the ancestors of modern crocodiles.

But there were many other kinds of reptiles as well, tens of thousands of them. And there were reptiles that would tower over any land-dwelling creatures alive today.

The greatest of the reptiles in this ancient world were the dinosaurs. They came in thousands of different varieties, some of them as small as monkeys or eagles, others as large

Crocodiles and snakes are reptiles, just as dinosaurs were, but they survived into modern times while the mighty dinosaurs did not.

as the largest whale. Dinosaurs dominated the face of the earth. Some were savage predators, with teeth like daggers and claws like spikes. Others were content to spend their lives eating plants, shielding themselves from predators by means of suits of natural armor or sharp spikes built into their flesh.

It's strange to think that the world could ever have been this way. When we look out our windows we see a land of lawns and highways, buildings and people. And yet this may be the very land over which dinosaurs once roamed.

The dinosaurs passed away long ago. The last *Tyrannosaurus rex* perished more than 60 million years ago. No one will ever see a *Brontosaurus* in the flesh or a *Diplodocus*, unless some method of time travel is developed. But we can travel back into the past by another method. Deep within the earth lie the remains that the dinosaurs left behind—their bones, footprints, and impressions in rock. We refer to these remains, and the remains of other, long-dead plants and animals, as fossils.

By studying fossils, we can make the world of the reptiles come alive, if only in our imaginations. To learn as much as they can about dinosaurs, scientists called paleontologists have been sifting through this fossil record for more than a hundred years. And every time a new dinosaur bone is unearthed, the age of reptiles becomes just a little more real.

Dinosaur tracks in a stream bed. By studying the imprints left by dinosaurs, we can learn a great deal about the creatures that made them.

(2)

The Story in the Bones

When was the first dinosaur fossil discovered?

That's difficult to say. Probably, human beings have been discovering dinosaur fossils for thousands of years without knowing what they were. Because no one even knew that dinosaurs had existed, the bones and footprints were thought to be something other than what they actually were. For instance, the first recorded discovery of dinosaur footprints was in the state of Massachusetts in 1802. For half a century afterward, they were believed to be the tracks of a giant bird. (In fact, many people regarded them as the tracks of "Noah's Raven," after the biblical story of the flood.) Some early dinosaur fossils were actually thought to be the remains of giant prehistoric humans, because the Bible makes references to the existence of giants in ancient times.

Then, two centuries ago, all of this began to change. People slowly began to accept the idea that animals that lived on the earth in past ages might have ceased to exist. They began to accept the idea of extinction.

Oddly, this was considered a radical notion. As recently as the eighteenth century, it was widely believed that the earth was only 6,000 years old. (In fact, some people still believe this today, although there is very little evidence in favor of this theory.) Sometime during the seventeenth century, Archbishop Ussher of Ireland calculated that God had created the earth on October 23, 4004 B.C. He based this on evidence he believed he had found in the Bible. If this were so—and many people once thought it was so—it would be difficult to believe that very many species would have had time to become extinct since the creation of the world.

And yet the fossils could not be ignored. Hardly a year went by when workers digging in quarries or mines did not uncover the fossilized remains of some animal that had died long ago—and most of these fossils bore only slight resemblance to animals living today. Obviously, they were different species altogether, species that existed no longer.

One of the greatest experts on animals both living and dead was Baron Georges Cuvier of France, who lived during the late eighteenth and early nineteenth centuries. When the immense skull of a strange-looking reptile was found in a mine in the Netherlands in 1770, it was inevitable that it would eventually find its way into Cuvier's hands. Cuvier correctly identified the skull as that of a giant marine reptile, an animal that must have lived in the ocean in prehistoric times. This animal was later given the name *Mosasaurus* by the British geologist William Conybeare. *Mosasaurus* is Latin for "Maas lizard." (The skull was found not far from the Maas River.) Cuvier later identified another fossil as that of a prehistoric flying reptile, which he called a *Pterodactyl* ("wing finger"). Though both of these creatures were giant prehistoric reptiles, they were not dinosaurs.

Dr. Gideon Mantell was a British physician who practiced in the first part of the nineteenth century. One day in 1822, while Mantell was visiting a patient, his wife went wandering

Pterodactyl was a prehistoric
flying reptile that was not a dinosaur.

around the countryside looking at rock formations. Both she and her husband were interested in fossils. When she spotted a tooth embedded in a piece of rock, she picked it up. Later she showed it to her husband.

He sensed immediately that it was something of importance. Though they did not realize it, the Mantells had just made the first known discovery of a dinosaur bone. (Remember, the *Mosasaurus* and *Pterodactyl*, though giant lizards, were not dinosaurs. And though such fossils had undoubtedly been discovered in earlier times, no one had realized their significance.)

Mantell sent the fossil to Cuvier, hoping that the Frenchman would be able to identify it. Alas, Cuvier declared that it was probably no more than the tooth of a rhinoceros!

But the doctor sensed that it was more than that. So he went to see England's leading fossil expert, Dean William Buckland of Oxford, and showed him the fossil. Buckland agreed with Cuvier. The fossil, he said, was of no particular importance.

Fortunately, Mantell refused to accept the judgment of these experts. In 1825, three years after the discovery of the fossil, Mantell was shown the tooth of a modern reptile known as an iguana. It bore a very strong resemblance to his fossil tooth. Here was the proof he needed! His fossil must be the tooth of an extinct reptile—a reptile at least as large as a rhinoceros. Mantell wanted to give his reptile the somewhat redundant name of *Iguanosaurus* ("iguana lizard"), but the geologist Conybeare convinced him to give it the more accurate name of *Iguanodon* ("iguana tooth"). When Mantell wrote Cuvier to tell him what he had concluded about the tooth, Cuvier admitted his mistake and agreed with Mantell's assessment of the fossil.

But was this the first dinosaur fossil ever identified? Not quite. During the period when Mantell was attempting to identify his fossil tooth, another fossil had fallen into the hands of William Buckland, the same William Buckland that Mantell had consulted at Oxford. It was the remains of the jaw and parts of the skeleton of a prehistoric animal. It had large, bladelike teeth, and Buckland identified the animal as having been a giant, meat-eating reptile. He named it *Megalosaurus* ("great lizard"). Like *Iguanodon*, *Megalosaurus* was a dinosaur.

Finally, in 1842, the English geologist Sir Richard Owen announced that the creatures identified by Mantell and Buckland must belong to an order of animals that had existed on the earth in great numbers many years ago. He called this order the *Dinosauria* ("terrible lizards")—dinosaurs. After millions of years, the ancient reptiles finally had a name!

Dinosaurs quickly captured the public imagination. Though many people probably thought of paleontology—the study of fossils—as a very dull science, concerned only with old bones, the idea that the earth was once populated by giant reptiles was an exciting one. There was a certain magic to the very word *dinosaur*.

In 1853, a number of the most famous paleontologists and geologists, including Sir Richard Owen, gathered at London's Crystal Palace. The scientists had been invited there to have dinner—inside a life-sized model of an *Iguanodon*!

Though "dinosaur-mania" began in England, it soon spread to the United States. The first dinosaur fossils identified in America came from South Dakota and Montana; they had been picked up in 1855 by Dr. Ferdinand V. Hayden, an early scientist-explorer of the West. Hayden carried them East,

***Iguanodon* was one of the first dinosaurs to be identified.**

Elasmosaurus was a prehistoric reptile
with a 25-foot-long (7.5-m) neck.

where he gave them to Dr. Joseph Leidy of the Academy of Natural Sciences in Philadelphia. Leidy studied the fossils and wrote a paper describing them in careful detail.

In 1858, a partial dinosaur skeleton was discovered in Haddonfield, New Jersey, practically in Leidy's backyard. Leidy studied it and concluded that it represented a new species of dinosaur, which he called *Hadrosaurus*.

With the intervention of the Civil War, the study of dinosaurs was forgotten in the United States for several years. After the war, however, paleontology came back with a vengeance.

The most important of the American "dinosaur hunters" were two men named Othniel Marsh and Edward Drinker Cope. Both were eminent paleontologists, and both were actively engaged in the search for significant new fossils in the latter half of the nineteenth century. It is ironic, then, that they disliked one another so intensely.

Apparently, the rivalry between Marsh and Cope began in 1870, when Cope assembled the skeleton of a prehistoric reptile with a 25-foot-long (7.5-m) neck, appropriately named *Elasmosaurus* ("ribbon reptile"). Marsh took one look at the skeleton and announced that Cope had put it together incorrectly, that the head had been placed at the wrong end of the skeleton!

Cope was furious, all the more so because it turned out that Marsh was right. The two paleontologists avoided one another for years afterward, each trying desperately to outdo the other in the discovery and identification of important fossils.

The greatest fossil beds in the United States were in the American West. (Although dinosaurs existed all over the earth, some areas were better for the preservation of fossils than others.) Marsh and Cope would each send expeditions into the deserts of Colorado and Wyoming, where hostile Indians and the hostile climate were as much a problem as the actual unearthing of the fossils. Supposedly, Cope himself was once captured by unfriendly Indians, who let him go only because of their fascination with his false teeth, an artifact of the white man's civilization they had never seen before.

The expeditions organized by Marsh and Cope did much to enhance our knowledge of the age of reptiles. Although the rivalry between the two men was probably an embarrassment to most scientists of the period, it may have driven the two of them to achieve far more than they would have otherwise.

Since that time, there have been many valuable fossil discoveries, in the American West and elsewhere. One skeleton, uncovered in Wyoming in 1908 by the great fossil hunter Charles Sternberg, included impressions of dinosaur flesh in the adjoining rock. This valuable discovery has helped us to imagine what dinosaur skin may actually have looked like, something that the bones alone cannot do.

Some finds, made mostly in Mongolia and France, have included fossilized dinosaur eggs. The most interesting thing about these eggs is that they are surprisingly small compared to the size of the adult dinosaurs. Some adult dinosaurs must have been more than 10,000 times larger than the newborn dinosaurs of their species.

The search for dinosaur fossils has continued to this very day. Recently, in Colorado, paleontologists unearthed the skeleton of what may have been the largest dinosaur that ever existed. (At least, it was the largest yet discovered.) Named *Ultrasaurus*, it must have stood some 50 or 60 feet (15 or 18 m) tall and weighed around 80 tons.

As remarkable as the discoveries of the past have been, however, it is likely that even more remarkable discoveries will be made in the future. And our knowledge of the age of dinosaurs will increase with every find.

(3)

The Origin of the Dinosaurs

Four billion years ago the planet earth was a barren chunk of rock orbiting the sun. There were no dinosaurs on the earth or mammals or even insects. There was no life at all.

We don't know exactly when the first living thing appeared, but whenever it did it was probably the direct descendant of a collection of atoms floating in the sea. (Atoms are the basic unit out of which nearly everything is made. You can imagine them as extremely tiny bits of matter, millions of times smaller than the smallest mote of dust.) These atoms were linked together into long, complicated chains we call molecules. The particular molecules we are talking about—the ones from which living organisms descended—would have had the ability to make copies of themselves. That would have been about the only thing that set them apart from other molecules, ones that had no potential for life. Because these particular molecules could make copies of themselves, there would have been a lot of them around.

They were not necessarily perfect at making copies of themselves, however, and so occasionally the copies were a little different from the originals. We call these imperfect copies mutations. Mutations are how living molecules came to be different from one another.

New types of living molecules kept appearing. Some of these molecules were bigger than others. Some had protective shells around them, to keep them from becoming damaged by things that were happening around them. Because these molecules were protected from their environment, they survived longer than molecules that were not protected. We can say, then, that they were *successful* molecules; in other words, they were good at what they did. The other molecules, the ones that weren't as good at protecting themselves, were less successful. The successful molecules thrived; the unsuccessful ones were destroyed or died out.

This process by which successful living organisms survive while unsuccessful organisms die out is called natural selection. It is still going on today, and not just in molecules. Natural selection takes place for all living organisms—animals and plants alike.

Mutation and natural selection combine to form the process called evolution. Even today, living creatures make "copies" of themselves, just as these primitive molecules did. Sometimes, copies are made that differ in some significant way from the originals. If these "incorrect" copies, these mutations, are more successful at surviving than the original, then eventually the new version will come to outnumber the original. A new kind of living organism will come to exist.

For this reason, living things are always changing. Few animals or insects or even the tiniest, simplest organisms that live on the earth today, including bacteria, are exactly like the ones that lived on earth millions of years ago. Mutations are constantly occurring; sometimes these mutations represent improvements over the original.

Scientists believe that we are the distant descendants of some of the molecules that floated in the ancient sea. This might sound strange, considering that we don't bear much resemblance to those molecules. And yet, the molecules of human flesh bear a strong resemblance to those of the earliest living organisms. All living organisms, from the first primitive, organic molecules to human beings, are put together in very similar ways. The main difference is that "higher" organisms such as human beings are much larger and more complex. And we became what we are through evolution.

The dinosaurs also descended from those ancient molecules. But before we examine how the "terrible lizards" evolved, let's first take a closer look at how evolution works.

Those organisms that are better equipped to survive will eventually outnumber those organisms that are not as well equipped to survive. This is the primary rule of evolution. However, just being able to survive is not enough. An organism must be able to survive in the particular environment in which it lives.

The environment is simply the sum total of all the things that surround or affect an organism—the terrain, the weather, other organisms, and so forth. For most of us, our environment is made up of buildings and plants and other people and occasional animals. We are well equipped to survive in such an environment. In fact, human beings are so adaptable that we can live in a wide variety of environments.

Not all of the earth's creatures are so lucky. An animal with a thick coat of fur, for instance, would be well equipped to live in a very cold environment but would fare poorly in the jungles of Peru. Similarly, an animal that ate grass in order to survive would get along fine in the great plains of the American Midwest but would not last long in a desert.

There are many different kinds of environments, and within each there are many different ways to survive. The word *ecological* refers to the manner in which different elements of an environment (ecology) interact with one another. An animal that survives in a particular way is said to occupy a particular ecological niche.

Only so many animals can occupy a single niche; sometimes there is only room for one. Suppose, for instance, that an animal survives by eating insects. There are only so many insects to go around. If too many animals try to occupy this niche, some of them are going to starve. Only those that are best at catching insects will survive.

Sometimes the environment changes, and ecological niches must change with it. If all insects suddenly disappeared from the face of the earth, for instance, the insect-eating niche would cease to exist as well. Animals that occupied that niche would have to find a new niche to fill, or they would die out just like the insects.

How does an animal find a new niche? A creature that is born with the ability to eat insects cannot suddenly start eating something else—plants, for instance. The animal probably isn't built for it. Only evolution can change an animal's niche. And evolution takes time. Fortunately, changes in the environment usually occur gradually. Living creatures have time to adapt.

The dinosaurs populated the earth for more than 100 million years. They must have occupied their niche very successfully. (Actually, dinosaurs occupied a wide variety of ecological niches.) In a moment, we'll see why they were so successful. But first let us take a look at the way scientists have divided the past, to give us a clearer understanding of it.

Paleontologists are interested in time, especially in how long ago various organisms lived and what organisms were alive at the same time. Therefore, they divide the past into a series of eras, according to what was alive then.

There are seven such eras, but it is only the last three that interest us here. These are the Paleozoic ("old life") era, the Mesozoic ("middle life") era, and the Cenozoic ("new life") era.

The Paleozoic began about 570 million years ago. Before the Paleozoic, life existed only in the oceans. The kinds of life that existed before the Paleozoic left very little behind in the way of fossils. During the Paleozoic, however, life emerged from the sea and spread across the land. This is the age during which reptiles first appeared.

The Mesozoic began about 225 million years ago. It was the age of dinosaurs; during the Mesozoic, giant reptiles populated practically the entire earth.

The Cenozoic began about 65 million years ago. If the Mesozoic was the age of dinosaurs, then the Cenozoic was the age of mammals. In fact, we are still in the Cenozoic today.

The three great eras are themselves divided up into smaller segments called periods. The Mesozoic, for instance, is divided up into the Triassic, Jurassic, and Cretaceous periods.

In the first part of the Paleozoic, when all life was in the ocean, the most advanced living organisms were the fishes. About half a billion years ago, however, a kind of fish existed that could live for short periods of time out of water. This was a type of fish that today we would call a lungfish. Ordinary fish do not have lungs, but the body of this lungfish contained a special bladder, a sort of balloon-like structure that could hold large amounts of air.

The lungfish probably tended to live in shallow pools of

water. This was its ecological niche. Other fish could not share this niche because the pools would occasionally dry up. When this happened the lungfish, who could continue to breathe, would use its fins to drag itself to another pool. Eventually, the fins evolved into legs. The air bladder evolved into a real lung. This new animal could live both in and out of water. It was what we would now call an amphibian.

The amphibians were so successful at occupying their particular ecological niche that they are still around today. Frogs and salamanders are amphibians.

During a portion of the Paleozoic that we refer to as the Carboniferous period, the amphibians were the dominant type of animal on the earth's surface. In fact, they were practically the only type of animal on the earth's surface. This was from about 345 million years ago to 280 million years ago.

There were problems, however, with the amphibian's ecological niche. For instance, if an amphibian's skin became completely dry, the animal would die. Therefore, an amphibian could not wander very far from water. This tended to restrict its movements. A creature not bound by this limitation would have a great advantage over the amphibians.

The first creatures to escape this limitation were the reptiles. They were direct descendants of the amphibians. In fact, the early reptiles were very much like amphibians, except that they had a thick, leathery skin that allowed them to remain on dry land indefinitely.

Because the reptiles could go places that the amphibians could not, this opened up a tremendous number of ecological niches that had not been available to living creatures before. In a short time, the reptiles occupied them all. When animals radiate (move outward) into a large number of ecological niches all at once, we refer to the process as radiative evolution, or adaptive radiation.

The last portion of the Paleozoic era is called the Permian period. During this period the reptiles were dominant. In a sense, the Permian marked the beginning of the age of reptiles, which lasted until the end of the Mesozoic era.

During the Permian a particular kind of reptile appeared, called the pelycosaur. There were many types of pelycosaurs, but what was important about them was that some of them may have had a means of controlling their body temperatures.

Why is this important? Well, the temperature of an animal's body must remain within a certain range or the animal will die. The body of a human being, for instance, usually remains at or close to 98.6° Fahrenheit (36° Celsius). (This is why you are considered sick if your body temperature is over 100°F.) Human beings and other mammals have a way of controlling this temperature. There are tiny "furnaces" within the cells of every mammal's body. These furnaces burn food for fuel and produce heat. If your body should become too warm, you sweat or pant. Sweating and panting are both methods of releasing heat from the body.

An animal that can control its temperature internally like this is said to be warm-blooded. An animal that is not able to control its body temperature internally is said to be cold-blooded.

Reptiles are cold-blooded. This does not mean that they are necessarily cold to the touch. It simply means that they have no "furnaces" within the body to keep them warm. In order to warm up, a reptile must lie in the sun until its body reaches a certain temperature. Once it has reached this temperature, it must scurry back into the shade, before it becomes too warm.

What made the pelycosaurs unusual, then, was that they may have had a method for controlling their body temperature. There were no "furnaces" within their bodies, but they had other ways.

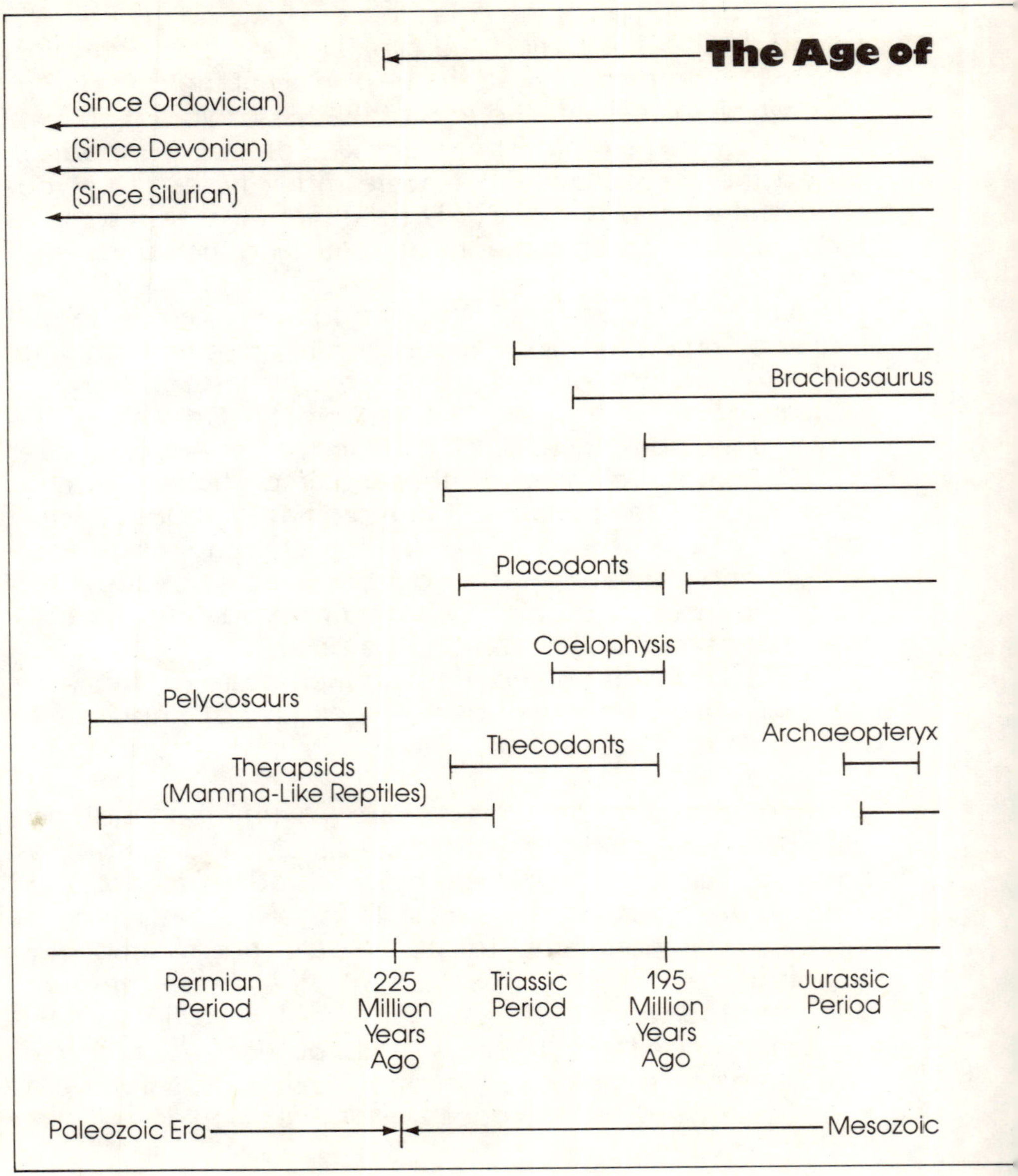
The Age of
(Since Ordovician)
(Since Devonian)
(Since Silurian)
Brachiosaurus
Placodonts
Coelophysis
Pelycosaurs
Thecodonts
Archaeopteryx
Therapsids
(Mamma-Like Reptiles)
Permian Period
225 Million Years Ago
Triassic Period
195 Million Years Ago
Jurassic Period
Paleozoic Era
Mesozoic

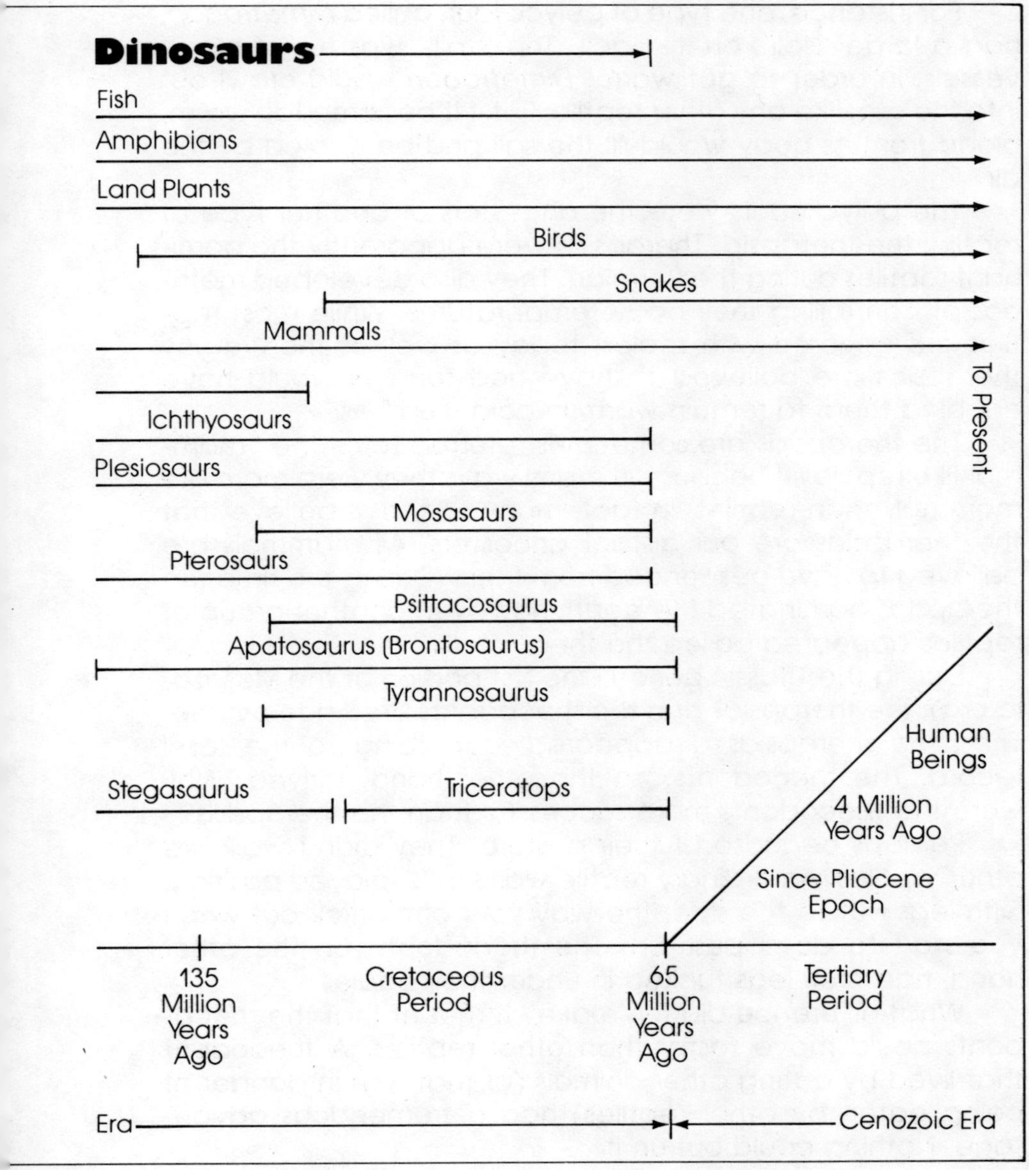

Dinosaurs
Fish
Amphibians
Land Plants
Birds
Snakes
Mammals
To Present
Ichthyosaurs
Plesiosaurs
Mosasaurs
Pterosaurs
Psittacosaurus
Apatosaurus (Brontosaurus)
Tyrannosaurus
Human Beings
Stegasaurus
Triceratops
4 Million Years Ago
Since Pliocene Epoch
135 Million Years Ago
Cretaceous Period
65 Million Years Ago
Tertiary Period
Era
Cenozoic Era

For instance, one type of pelycosaur, called *Dimetrodon*, had a large "sail" on its back. This "sail" was full of blood vessels. In order to get warm, *Dimetrodon* would crawl out into the sun, like any other reptile. But if it became too warm, blood from its body would fill the sail and be cooled by the air.

The pelycosaurs were the ancestors of another type of reptile, the therapsid. Therapsids were apparently the dominant reptiles during the Permian. They also developed methods of controlling their body temperatures. While most reptiles are covered with scales, today as well as then, many therapsids are believed to have had fur; this would have enabled them to remain warm in cold weather.

The therapsids are sometimes referred to as the "mammal-like reptiles," because in many ways they were more like mammals than reptiles. In fact, many scientists believe that the therapsids are our distant ancestors. All mammals are believed to have descended from them. During the time the therapsids dominated the earth, however, another group of reptiles appeared called the thecodonts.

During the Triassic period (the first portion of the Mesozoic era), the therapsids and the thecodonts lived side by side. Then the therapsids disappeared, according to the fossil record. The thecodonts, on the other hand, thrived. Why were the thecodonts more successful than the therapsids?

Perhaps because of their posture. They didn't walk like other reptiles. An ordinary reptile walks in a splayed position, with legs out to the side, the way your arms stick out when you start to do a push-up. The thecodonts, on the other hand, had their legs tucked in under their bodies.

What difference did this make? It meant that the thecodonts could move faster than other reptiles. A thecodont that lived by eating other animals (or that was in danger of being eaten by other reptiles) had a tremendous advantage. Nothing could outrun it.

Dimetrodon had a large "sail" on its back that might have been used to help it keep cool in the hot sun. The drawing (over) shows *Dimetrodon* with other reptiles of the Permian period.

With time, some thecodonts developed other improvements in their posture. They began to stand up straight. And they began to stand on only two legs instead of four. They became bipedal ("two-legged").

By the time this happened, however, they were already well on their way to becoming something other than thecodonts. They were becoming dinosaurs.

(4)

The Biggest and the Fiercest

What were dinosaurs?

That's a tougher question than you might think. The answer depends in part on whom you ask. Some paleontologists might reply that there were no such things as "dinosaurs" at all.

What? No dinosaurs? Isn't this a book about dinosaurs?

Well, yes. And everybody knows what dinosaurs were. Everybody except the scientists who study them, that is.

For one thing, the term *dinosaur* was invented quite a long time ago, as you saw in the second chapter. When Sir Richard Owen suggested that a few fossils be considered as a special group of animals called the *Dinosauria*, little was known about these animals. Now we know a lot more. We know, for example, that what were once considered dinosaurs are actually two separate and very different groups of reptiles called the ornithischians and the saurischians.

But let's back up for a minute. In the last chapter we saw that the thecodonts were the dominant reptiles during the Triassic period (the first part of the Mesozoic era). The theco-

Compsognathus, possibly the smallest dinosaur that ever lived, was no bigger than a turkey. It is shown here (left foreground) with some flying reptiles and primitive birds.

donts, in fact, were the first members of a larger group of reptiles called the archosaurs—the "ruling reptiles."

By the end of the Triassic, four more types of archosaurs had come along: the crocodilia (ancestors of the modern crocodiles), the pterosaurs (flying reptiles), and the two types of dinosaurs mentioned above. All of these were direct descendants of the thecodonts. It was the archosaurs that dominated the earth during the Mesozoic. And the dinosaurs were the dominant archosaurs.

One of the earliest dinosaurs that we are aware of is *Coelophysis*. *Coelophysis* was the first of a group of dinosaurs called the coelurosaurs. Lightly built, hollow-boned, and fast-moving, the coelurosaurs looked somewhat like birds. In fact, there is some evidence that certain coelurosaurs might have had feathers! We'll take a closer look at this in Chapter Seven.

Coelophysis poses an interesting problem to paleontologists. We know that most reptiles lay eggs rather than giving birth to live young. Yet an adult *Coelophysis* skeleton has been discovered with a young *Coelophysis* skeleton inside it! Does this mean that the *Coelophysis* in question was pregnant? Or was the creature instead a cannibal? The skeleton within the skeleton seems almost too large to be an unborn *Coelophysis*. And yet it is completely undamaged, which makes it seem unlikely that it had been eaten for dinner. No one has yet come up with a satisfactory answer as to what the young *Coelophysis* skeleton was doing inside the adult *Coelophysis*'s body.

Another of the coelurosaurs, *Compsognathus*, may have been the smallest dinosaur that ever lived. It was no bigger than an average-sized turkey.

The coelurosaurs were saurischians. (We saw a moment ago that all dinosaurs fell into two orders, the saurischians and the ornithischians.) The name *saurischian* means "lizard-hipped." This simply meant that the saurischians had pretty much the same kind of hips as any other reptile. The name *ornithischian*, on the other hand, means "bird hipped;" as you might guess from this, the ornithischians had hips very much like those of birds. (You'll notice that we'll be talking about birds a great deal as we discuss dinosaurs. The reason for this is that the dinosaurs are the direct ancestors of birds. In fact, there are some authorities who argue that birds should be classed as a type of dinosaur! We'll talk more about this later.)

Basically, there were two types of saurischians. These were the theropods ("beast-footed") and the sauropods ("lizard-footed"). Obviously, their names refer to the appearance of their feet. Both types of saurischians appeared in the late Triassic and early Jurassic periods. (The coelurosaurs were theropods.)

The theropods were carnivores, or meat-eating animals. For this reason, they are sometimes referred to as carnosaurs. What they ate, in large part, were other dinosaurs. At the height of their success, the theropods included some of the most terrifying predators ever to stalk the face of the earth.

One of the earliest meat-eating dinosaurs that we know of was *Megalosaurus*, who, you may recall, was the first dinosaur ever named. Judging from the fossil record, *Megalosaurus* must have been a particularly successful dinosaur. It could grow to 25 feet (7.5 m) long and had teeth like serrated knives.

Possibly the most dangerous carnosaur of the Jurassic period was *Allosaurus*. *Allosaurus* had powerful legs and could spring unexpectedly on its victims.

Probably the best known of the theropods was *Tyrannosaurus rex*. *Tyrannosaurus* lived in the late Cretaceous period, at the end of the age of dinosaurs. Its name means "king of the tyrant lizards," and it may have been the largest carnivore ever to walk the earth. It stood 18 feet (5.4 m) high and

Tyrannosaurus rex, a dinosaur of the late Cretaceous period, must have been a fearsome predator.

had a body that could reach 50 feet (15 m) in length. With a weight of perhaps 8 tons and teeth that may have been as much as 6 inches (15 cm) long, it is little wonder that *Tyrannosaurus* is thought to have been a fearsome predator.

Surprisingly, however, because of its great bulk, *Tyrannosaurus* was probably also very slow. Most likely, it fed largely on carrion—the meat of animals that were already dead—and on other heavy, slow-moving dinosaurs trapped by their own bulk.

One of the great mysteries about *Tyrannosaurus* concerns its arms. They were very short, not even as long as human arms and ridiculously small considering *Tyrannosaurus*'s tremendous size. They would seem to be quite useless, compared to its mouth and powerful feet. What were they for? No one knows. It has been suggested that it used them to pick its teeth after a meal, though this is unlikely, as they would not have reached as far as its mouth. Perhaps the best suggestion so far is that it used the arms to keep its balance while standing up; otherwise it might have fallen forward on its face. But this still fails to explain why the arms were so small.

The other basic type of saurischian was the sauropod. Sauropods were all herbivorous ("plant-eating"). They were the largest of the dinosaurs. In fact, they were almost certainly the largest land-dwelling creatures ever to live on the earth. One of the first sauropods discovered was named *Cetiosaurus*—"whale lizard"—because of its great size. The name is appropriate because the largest of the sauropods, *Brachiosaurus*, was about the same size as today's giants of the sea, the blue whales.

Just as *Tyrannosaurus rex* is probably the best known of the theropods, *Brontosaurus* is probably the best known of the sauropods. (Actually, the paleontologist's term for *Brontosaurus* is *Apatosaurus*, but we'll refer to it here by its

Brontosaurus (above and over) was about 70 feet (21 m) long and weighed 30 tons.

more familiar name.) The average *Brontosaurus* was about 70 feet (21 m) long and weighed perhaps 30 tons. Unlike the theropods, *Brontosaurus* (and the other sauropods) stood on four legs. Probably, this was to accommodate its tremendous bulk.

Brontosaurus was by no means the largest of the sauropods. *Diplodocus*, though lighter than *Brontosaurus*, attained lengths of up to 90 feet (27 m). Most of this length was in its incredibly long neck and slender tail. *Diplodocus* had an extremely small head in relation to the rest of its body.

Brachiosaurus was just about the largest creature ever to walk the earth—or, rather, the heaviest. (*Diplodocus* was longer. And *Ultrasaurus* may have been larger still, but we don't know that much about it yet.) It weighed an estimated 50 tons and was 40 feet (12 m) tall. Most of this height came from a rather unusual feature: *Brachiosaurus*'s front legs were longer than its rear legs. In most dinosaurs the situation was precisely the reverse. Consider *Tyrannosaurus rex*, for example.

The huge weight of the sauropods raises some interesting questions. Why were they so large? And more importantly, how could they be so large?

Look at the animals on the earth today. The largest land-dwelling animal is the elephant, and elephants are only a fraction of the size of the larger sauropods. The only animals alive today comparable in size to *Brachiosaurus* are the blue whales, and they live in water.

There's an important difference between land-dwelling animals and water-dwelling animals. Water-dwelling animals don't have to support their full weight. The water supports it for them.

A whale, as heavy as it is, is nearly weightless as long as it remains in the water. The moment the whale finds itself on land, however, it is doomed. It cannot move or even breathe. It is crushed by its own weight.

How did the sauropods escape this terrible doom? For years, paleontologists believed that they did it by living in the water. Because most sauropod fossils were discovered in the vicinity of ancient bodies of water, it was assumed that dinosaurs such as *Brachiosaurus* and *Diplodocus* spent most of their time splashing around through lakes and rivers, with only their necks (or sometimes only their nostrils) sticking up into the air. Thus, the water could have served the double purpose of supporting the creatures' weight and hiding them from predators such as *Allosaurus* and *Tyrannosaurus*.

Now, however, many paleontologists have come to doubt this picture of sauropod life. They suspect that sauropods lived most of their lives on dry land. After all, the fact that sauropod skeletons tend to be found near water doesn't necessarily mean that all sauropods lived near water. It may just mean that lakes and rivers were a good place for fossils to be preserved. (Most dinosaur fossils formed when the remains of a dinosaur sank into the soft mud at the bottom of a lake or river, where they were preserved for millions of years. If a dinosaur died on dry land, its remains would simply have rotted away.)

Most paleontologists now believe that the sauropods were simply masterpieces of biological engineering, built as sturdily as modern suspension bridges. (In *Diplodocus*, this was literally true. The spine of this sauropod was curved in almost exactly the same way as the suspension portion of a large bridge.) To support such tremendous weight, the sauropod's legs must have contained nearly solid columns of bone. The rest of the bones in the sauropod's body, on the other hand, must have been mostly hollow, to keep the creature's total weight to a minimum.

This brings us to the second question concerning the sauropod's weight. Why were these creatures so heavy?

You'll recall that we said earlier that reptiles are cold-blooded. This means simply that they have no internal control over their body temperatures. In most instances, a reptile must use solar energy to become warm. That is, it must lie in the sun and absorb the sun's heat.

A small reptile, however, will gain and lose the sun's heat much faster than a large reptile. The bulk of a dinosaur—especially a dinosaur as large as the sauropods were—would act as a kind of heat trap. It would take a large dinosaur a long time to become warm, because there would be so much bulk to heat. But it would also take a long time for that dinosaur to become cold again. *Brachiosaurus*, for instance, would have to lie in the sun for several days in order to raise its body temperature by one degree! But once *Brachiosaurus* was warm, it would stay warm for a long time.

The sauropod's great size, therefore, helped protect it against sudden changes in temperature. Since the sauropods were not very fast-moving and could not scurry for protection in the event of sudden heat or cold, as smaller reptiles can, this was very important. And it was not just true of the sauropods, either. It was also true of the theropods and the ornithischians. In fact, many dinosaurs were large animals. The sauropods were simply the largest of the large. All dinosaurs, therefore, tended to retain heat. By simply being big, they were able to overcome the disadvantages of being cold-blooded.

There are some paleontologists, however, who argue that the dinosaurs were not cold-blooded at all, that they were warm-blooded, like mammals. If this is so, it may mean that dinosaurs were not reptiles in the usual sense but a variety of reptile that does not yet even have a name.

So far no one has been able to come up with conclusive proof on either side of the argument. Were the dinosaurs cold-blooded or warm-blooded? No one knows for sure. Perhaps, in the end, it doesn't even really matter. Because of their huge size, their blood was probably warm most of the time, anyway.

(5)

Plate and Armor, Crests and Horns

If the saurischians were the largest and most frightening of the dinosaurs, then the ornithischians were the oddest. Some, for instance, were constructed like tanks, with armor plating and built-in weapons. Others had bizarre crests on top of their heads and strange spines on their backs.

Just as the saurischians divide up into two basic types, the theropods and the sauropods, so the ornithischians can be broken up into four different types.

The first of these were the ornithopods. No one is sure where the ornithopods came from. Judging from the fossil record, it seems as if they materialized out of thin air. Certainly, they must have descended from the thecodonts, just as the saurischian dinosaurs did. But which ones? None that we've discovered so far, it would appear.

The ornithopods seemed to have appeared in the late Triassic period. They were just about the only ornithischians that tended to walk on two legs. Of the first ornithopods, the one that we know the most about is *Fabrosaurus*, a small dinosaur probably only about 3 feet (0.9 m) long.

Once we get into the mid-Cretaceous period, however, the ornithopods become more interesting, and we know more about them. For instance, a later ornithopod, *Hypsilophodon*, bore a certain resemblance to the modern kangaroo. Larger than *Fabrosaurus*, it was still no more than 5 feet (1.5 m) long. It must have walked in a kind of forward crouch, with its head only about 2 feet (0.6 m) off the ground.

Iguanodon, which resembled *Hypsilophodon*, though it was larger, was also an ornithopod. You'll recall that *Iguanodon* received its name from Dr. Gideon Mantell, who thought that its teeth resembled those of an iguana.

Like all ornithischians, *Iguanodon* was herbivorous. It ate only plants. Even so, it was much bigger than meat-eating theropods such as *Megalosaurus*. It generally achieved lengths of around 30 feet (0.9 m) and weights of roughly 7 tons.

Like the theropods, *Iguanodon* was bipedal. That is, it walked on two legs. It also had a large spiked claw sticking out from each of its thumbs. There is some debate about what these claws were used for. Some paleontologists believe that they were a weapon, used for defense against predators. Others suspect that they were used to attract members of the opposite sex.

Possibly the most interesting group of ornithopods were the hadrosaurs, or duck-billed dinosaurs. The hadrosaurs occupied roughly the same ecological niche as antelopes and similar animals do in modern-day Africa. Hadrosaurs would feed in herds, keeping a sharp eye out for predators. What makes the hadrosaurs particularly fascinating to study are the odd crests some of them had on top of their heads.

No one knows what these crests were for. As usual, though, there is no shortage of theories. The crests came in all shapes and sizes; most were hollow and were directly connected to the dinosaur's nostrils. One theory is that they were a kind of snorkel that allowed the animal to breathe while it hid underwater from carnosaurs. This theory falls apart, however, when we consider that there is no opening at the top of the crest for the air to pass through.

Another theory is that the crests were more an aqualung than a snorkel. According to this theory, air was stored inside the crest so that a hadrosaur hiding underwater would have an extra supply of air when the air in its lungs ran out. The problem with this is that the hadrosaur's lungs could hold much more air than the crest could. The extra air in the crest would have been used up in a few seconds—hardly long enough to make having the crest worthwhile.

Perhaps the best explanation yet given for the hadrosaur crest is that it was a "second nose." Air that passed in through the hadrosaur's nostrils would have spent a great deal of time in the crest before it reached the hadrosaur's lungs. If there were special smelling organs in the crest, this would have given the hadrosaur an excellent sense of smell, thus allowing a hadrosaur to smell a *Tyrannosaurus rex* or other carnosaur approaching from a great distance. The hadrosaur might then have been able to warn the rest of the herd, giving it adequate time to flee.

Another possibility is that the crest was a loudspeaker, able to intensify the sound of the hadrosaur's bellow (assuming that the hadrosaur could bellow). In this way, individual hadrosaurs could have kept in touch with other hadrosaurs from the same herd. The entire herd, therefore, would have had a better chance of sticking together and thus a better chance of defending itself against carnosaurs.

All of this fits in with other things that we know about hadrosaurs—for instance, that they had a very good sense of hearing and excellent eyesight. All in all, the hadrosaurs were extremely advanced reptiles.

This drawing shows some additional dinosaurs of the late Cretaceous period, including hadrosaurs, or duck-billed dinosaurs (*Edmontosaurus*) at right, hooded dinosaurs (*Corthosaurus*) in the swamp at left, and armored dinosaurs (*Palaeoscenus*) in the center foreground. The ostrichlike dinosaurs in the background are *Struthiomimus*.

CHAS. R. KNIGHT

Despite its upright "plates" and spiked tail, *Stegosaurus* was probably not a formidable enemy. It had a brain only the size of an apple.

The second line of ornithischians were the stegosaurs. The largest and best known of the stegosaurs was *Stegosaurus* itself. At its largest, *Stegosaurus* was about 25 feet (7.5 m) long and weighed 4 tons.

What was most striking about *Stegosaurus* was that it had a series of plates running along its back. Nobody is sure what these plates were for. As a matter of fact, nobody even knows exactly how *Stegosaurus* "wore" these plates.

The best guess is that they stood upright on its back in two rows, side by side. Did they give *Stegosaurus* protection against its enemies? Maybe. But if so, how? They left most of the creature's soft organs open to attack by theropods. There was no apparent way that *Stegosaurus* could use the plates for weapons. At least one paleontologist has suggested that the plates were actually laid flat against *Stegosaurus*'s flesh, rather than standing upright. This isn't very likely, though. Another possible explanation for the plates is that they helped remove heat from *Stegosaurus*'s body, like *Dimetrodon*'s sail.

As for weapons, *Stegosaurus* had something much better than upright plates. It had a series of spikes on its tail, each about a yard (0.9 m) in length. These must have presented a frightening spectacle to any animal that might have decided to pick a fight with a *Stegosaurus*. One swish of its tail and the spikes would have become embedded in the flesh of an attacker.

As destructive as its tail might have been, *Stegosaurus* was probably not a very formidable enemy. It appears to have been a rather stupid dinosaur. It had an extremely small head and a brain the size of an apple. When *Stegosaurus* was first studied by paleontologists, it was noted that it had a large chamber in its spine.

All in all, the stegosaurs were among the least successful dinosaurs. They died out in the early Cretaceous, the only major type of dinosaur to disappear before the end of the Mesozoic.

At about the time the stegosaurs disappeared, another branch of ornithischians came onto the scene, the ankylosaurs. Like the stegosaurs, the ankylosaurs were armored dinosaurs. Many of them had spikes on their tails. Some had solid plates set all across their backs.

Was the entrance of the ankylosaurs at a time when the stegosaurs were dying out a coincidence? Did the stegosaurs die out because the ankylosaurs did a better job of occupying the same ecological niche? Or did the ankylosaurs come to occupy the niche because the stegosaurs had died out? We don't know.

In some ways, the ankylosaurs were much like armadillos are today, only much larger. They were harmless plant-eaters, protected from their enemies by a nearly solid shell of armor. Their bellies were soft and unprotected, but any predator that tried to flip them over had to contend with the spikes on their backs and tails. Like *Stegosaurus,* some of these ankylosaurs could use their tails as a fighter might use a club or a mace.

The last group of ornithischian were the ceratopsians. The ceratopsians were extremely successful dinosaurs. Like the stegosaurs and ankylosaurs, they were armored and ate plants. The most striking attribute of the ceratopsian was its large rhinoceros-like horn.

The ceratopsians may have descended from a dinosaur called *Psittacosaurus*—"parrot lizard." *Psittacosaurus,* an early ornithipod, got its name because the front section of its skull was narrowed into the shape of a parrot's beak. *Psittacosaurus* probably used its beak for picking ripe fruit off trees.

One of the ceratopsians was *Protoceratops. Protoceratops* is especially interesting because it was the first dinosaur to be discovered (in fossilized skeletal form) along with its

Protoceratops with its eggs.

Triceratops was a horned dinosaur
of the late Cretaceous period.
Despite its combative look,
it was a plant-eating dinosaur.

own eggs, in Outer Mongolia in 1922. Apparently the ceratopsians that had laid these eggs had existed in the late Cretaceous, not long before dinosaurs disappeared from the face of the earth.

Protoceratops was a fairly small ceratopsian, about 6 feet (1.8 m) in length, and it had no horn. It did, however, have a feature in common with most other ceratopsians—a frill that covered its neck and the top of its skull. This frill was a kind of bony shell that the ceratopsians wore on their heads, extending back to their shoulders. It served as an anchor for the strong muscles in the ceratopsian neck and also as a protective shield for the vulnerable neck and shoulders.

The most familiar of the ceratopsians was *Triceratops,* a giant horned dinosaur of the late Cretaceous. *Triceratops* grew to lengths of 30 feet (9 m) or so and weighed 7 tons. It had thick, strong hooves and a short, stubby tail. On its head were three horns, two long ones and a short one. The head itself was enormous, more than 7 feet (2.1 m) long.

Triceratops generally traveled in herds. It is not hard to imagine how unappetizing a herd of *Triceratops* must have looked to a hungry theropod. With its great size, great numbers, thick armor, and sharp horns, *Triceratops* would have caused even *Tyrannosaurus rex* to think twice before considering it as a potential meal. For this reason, *Triceratops* was one of the most successful of all dinosaurs. It was also probably one of the last dinosaurs to disappear at the end of the Mesozoic.

(6) The Rest of the Reptiles

The Mesozoic is often referred to as the age of reptiles, and not without reason. Reptiles occupied almost every available ecological niche. They were the most successful form of animal that had yet evolved, with the possible exception of the insect.

Thus far, however, we have looked chiefly at the dinosaurs. Yet there were other forms of reptile, every bit as interesting and spectacular, living at the same time as the dinosaur. In this chapter we'll take a look at a few of those.

We saw earlier that dinosaurs belonged to a larger group of reptiles called the archosaurs, or "ruling reptiles." Another branch of the archosaurians were the thecodonts, which we talked about in Chapter Three.

Living alongside these reptiles, however, was yet another kind of archosaur, the crocodilians. We don't really need to say much about these because they are the only group of archosaurs to survive into the present day (as the crocodiles, among other species). We can note, however, that while present-day crocodiles have been known to grow as long as

30 feet (9 m), crocodiles from the distant past grew to considerably greater lengths, sometimes as long as a *Triceratops*!

The last type of archosaur was the pterosaur. These were flying reptiles, huge batlike creatures that soared along on the wind, attaining sizes that no modern bird even approaches.

The pterosaurs may have descended from a reptile called *Podopteryx* ('wing foot'') or some other closely related reptile. *Podopteryx* was about the size of a mouse and occupied pretty much the same ecological niche as the modern flying squirrel. It was built like a tiny hang glider, with a scaled webbing draped around its limbs. This webbing served the function of a simple wing. It allowed *Podopteryx* to glide from branch to branch in the forest, never having to touch the ground.

Of the pterosaurs that descended from *Podopteryx*, the most familiar is *Pteranodon*. *Pteranodon* had a wingspread of some 20 feet (6 m) but a body no larger than a turkey. In fact, *Pteranodon* was nearly all wing.

Still, it was amazingly large for a flying animal. How did it support its weight in the air? How did it get off the ground?

There are certain physical limits to the size of a flying creature. The heavier a flying animal is, the larger its wings have to be. But the larger the wings, the heavier the animal is. Above a certain size, the wings become so heavy that they cannot even support themselves.

The larger *Pteranodons* got around this limit by becoming extremely light for their size. An ordinary bird blown up to the size of a large *Pteranodon* would weigh about 200 pounds (90 kg). *Pteranodon* weighed only about 35 pounds (15.75 kg). The secret of its light weight was in its hollow skeleton. Only about 30 percent of its skeleton was solid. The rest was filled with tiny air sacs.

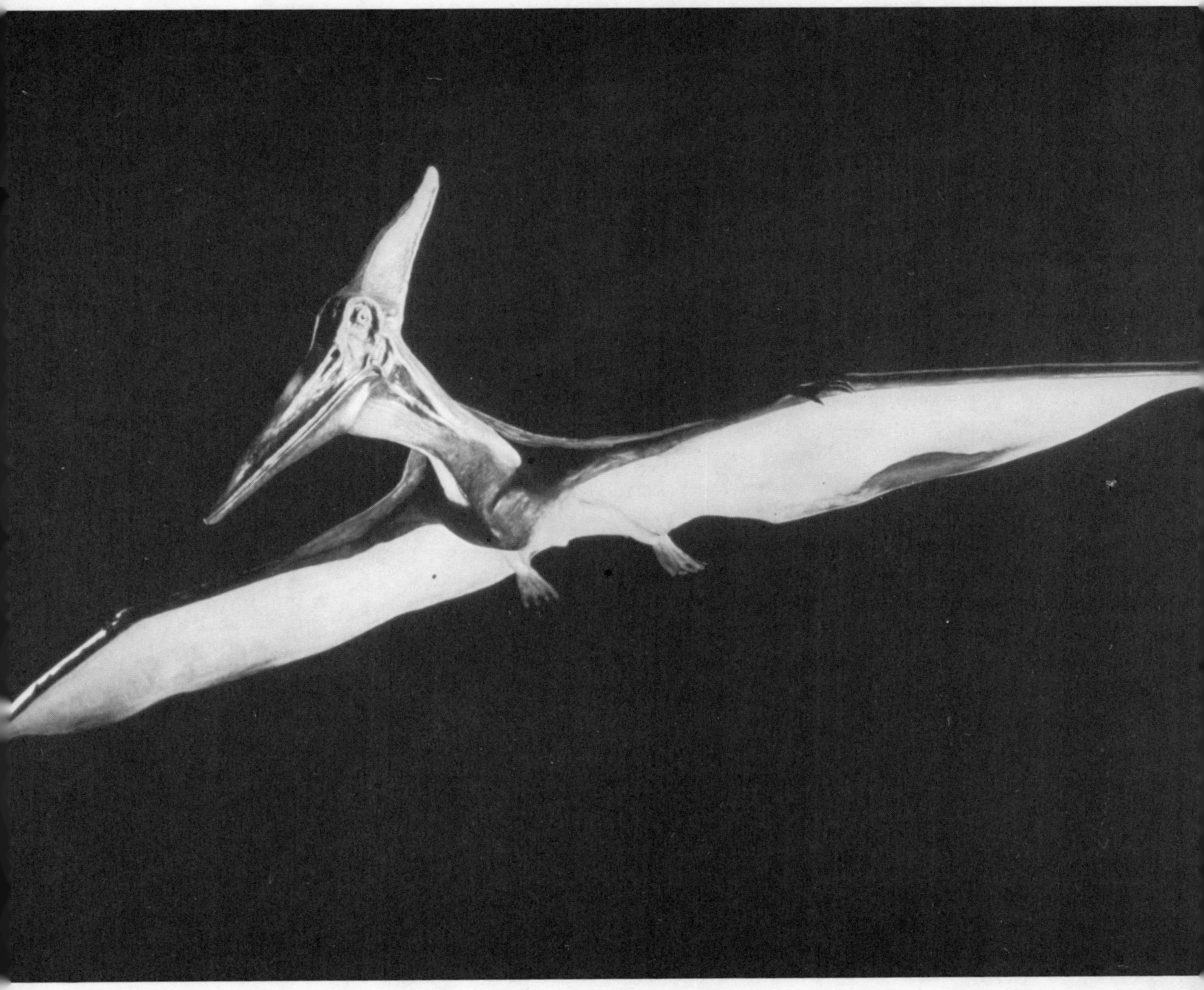

Pteranodon was a flying reptile
with a 20-foot (6-m) wingspread.

Still, paleontologists believed for a long time that *Pteranodon* was as large as a flying creature could possibly become. Nothing could ever have been larger and still flown.

They were quite wrong. In 1972, the bones of a giant flying reptile were discovered in Big Bend National Park in western Texas. The wingspan (the distance from the tip of one wing to the tip of the other) of this creature must have been nearly 40 feet (12 m)—twice as big as *Pteranodon*'s!

The man who discovered this flying reptile named it *Quetzalcoatlus*, after the Aztec god Quetzalcoatl, who supposedly took the form of a flying serpent. Because that name is rather difficult to pronounce, however, the creature is often just referred to as the Texas pterosaur.

The Texas pterosaur has caused paleontologists and other scientists to revise most of their notions about how animals fly. If *Pteranodon* represented a marvelous piece of aerodynamic engineering, then *Quetzalcoatlus* is nothing short of astonishing.

Another question that scientists ask about the pterosaurs is how they got off the ground. These reptiles were built for gliding. Once they got their broad wings on top of a gentle breeze, they could stay afloat for days at a time. But how did they get up into the breeze in the first place?

They couldn't have been very good at flapping their wings, the way that birds get up into the air. It has been suggested that they launched themselves by plunging from the tops of trees or diving off cliffs, but these possibilities seem rather unlikely. At one time it was believed that they never even touched the ground, preferring to spend their rest time hanging upside down from limbs and cliffsides, rather like bats. Paleontologists have begun to doubt this, however.

Another interesting feature of *Pteranodon* was the sharp crest on top of its skull, which may have acted as a kind of aerial brake. When turned into the wind, the crest could, have slowed *Pteranodon* down sufficiently for a safe landing. Yet other pterosaurs got along just fine without this crest. And *Pteranodon*'s neck bones seemed to have been locked in such a way that its neck would not have rotated very easily. Perhaps the crests were simply a way of telling male *Pteranodons* from female *Pteranodons*.

For many years there was a debate among paleontologists as to whether pterosaurs had scales, like ordinary lizards, or fur, like mammals (although the pterosaurs were definitely reptiles). This question was finally settled in 1971 when the skeleton of a pterosaur was discovered surrounded by the fossilized remains of hair. Apparently, pterosaurs were entirely covered with fur, except on their tails.

That finishes our look at the archosaurs. There were, however, other reptiles at large during the Mesozoic, and some of these were every bit as impressive as their archosaurian relatives. Some even lived in the ocean.

We can refer to these seagoing reptiles as marine reptiles and divide them up into three main groups: the ichthyosaurs, the plesiosaurs, and the mosasaurs.

The ichthyosaurs were a lot like dolphins. They had long, sleek bodies, flippers, and pointed snouts. They also had sharp, vicious-looking teeth.

Where did the ichthyosaurs come from? There is nothing in the fossil record to indicate that they came from anywhere at all, but certainly they must have descended from land-dwelling reptiles, the same way that whales and dolphins descended from land-dwelling mammals.

There is even the possibility that the ichthyosaurs were a separate line of evolution from other reptiles! This means that they would have descended from amphibians just as ordinary reptiles did, but they would have done it independently, without being related to any other kinds of reptiles. This is only theory, of course, and is not widely accepted.

Ichthyosaurs and plesiosaurs were reptiles that lived in the sea during the Mesozoic era.

The second kind of marine reptile was the plesiosaur. If ichthyosaurs were a lot like dolphins, plesiosaurs were more like giant turtles (though they were not closely related to turtles, which also existed in prehistoric times). The plesiosaurs descended from a group of early Triassic reptiles called the nothosaurs. Nothosaurs lived both in the water and on the shore. Plesiosaurs, on the other hand, spent all their time in the water.

William Buckland, who gave *Megalosaurus* its name, once described *Plesiosaurus* as a turtle with a snake strung through it. The description is a good one. Plesiosaurs had long, thin necks and fairly thick bodies, with paddles attached, paddles that looked a lot like those on a turtle. One plesiosaur, called *Elasmosaurus*, had a neck 23 feet (6.9 m) long! Why it needed a neck this long is hard to say. Probably, it was used for catching fish. Another type of plesiosaur, *Pliosaurus*, had a 13-foot (3.9-m) skull. This was the largest head of any known reptile.

The third type of marine reptile was the mosasaur. The mosasaurs appeared in the late Cretaceous and therefore were not around very long before the age of reptiles ended. They were the largest lizards ever, bearing a strong resemblance to the monitor lizard of today. They propelled themselves through the water with short paddles along the sides of their bodies and a large flattened tail.

Mosasaurs were predators. They probably ate anything that they could catch, including shellfish, which they must have crunched open in their powerful jaws, spitting out the parts that they couldn't digest.

You'll recall that the dominant form of reptile before the archosaurs came along were the therapsids, sometimes referred to as the "mammal-like reptiles." What happened to the therapsids?

After the dinosaurs appeared, the therapsids apparently died out, but they left behind their descendants, the mammals. Mammals came into existence in the late Triassic, which means that they lived side by side with the dinosaurs for tens of millions of years.

Quite possibly the dinosaurs didn't even know they were there, which is how the mammals managed to survive. They were very small animals, resembling the modern shrew. Some of them may even have lived in holes in the ground, burrowing into the earth as protection against predators. Probably, they were nocturnal creatures—that is, they came out mostly at night, when the larger animals were asleep.

The mammals existed like this right through the remainder of the Mesozoic. Then, suddenly, the dinosaurs vanished. Thousands of ecological niches opened up, and the mammals radiated into them. The age of reptiles was over. The age of mammals had begun.

It is interesting to wonder what would have happened if the dinosaurs had never come along. The therapsids occupied most of the ecological niches in the Permian and early Triassic periods. Perhaps when the mammals arrived they would have slowly taken over these niches—if the dinosaurs hadn't moved into them first.

The Mesozoic might have been the age of mammals. Human beings might have evolved 100 million years earlier than they did. It has even been suggested that if it hadn't been for the dinosaurs, the first human being might have landed on the moon sometime during the Cretaceous era.

Or maybe not. Maybe if there had been no dinosaurs, the mammals that evolved from the therapsids might have been completely different kinds of animals. During the Mesozoic, the mammals were forced to occupy a pretty narrow ecological niche. In order to fill that niche successfully, they had to become quick and intelligent just to survive. If it

Most mammals of the late Triassic
were small creatures that resembled
the modern shrew, shown here.

weren't for the dinosaurs, the mammals might have been slow and dumb, and intelligent creatures such as human beings might never have evolved at all.

It may be better that things happened just the way they did. Nature usually knows best.

(7)

The End of the Age of Reptiles

It would be nice to say that the story of the dinosaurs had a happy ending. But it didn't. Sixty-five million years ago, the dinosaurs vanished from the face of the earth. Not one survived. And no one knows why.

As the Cretaceous drew to a close, the dinosaurs were thriving as never before. Thousands of different species roamed the earth, some of them quite spectacular. And then they were gone.

Why the dinosaurs disappeared has puzzled paleontologists for nearly a century and a half and may go on puzzling them for at least that long into the future. Maybe they will never find a satisfactory answer.

The dinosaurs were very successful at occupying their particular ecological niches. There is no evidence that they were thrown out of these niches by other animals. The mammals offered them no particular competition. And yet the dinosaurs died out completely at the end of the Mesozoic and the mammals did not.

Why?

There must be hundreds of theories, but none explains everything about this so-called Great Cretaceous Extinction. Some of the theories are downright silly—that the dinosaurs died of boredom, that there was no room for them on Noah's Ark, or that the entire species had become old and senile, for example.

One of the more serious suggestions is that the mammals killed off the dinosaurs by eating their eggs. And yet dinosaurs and mammals lived side by side for most of the Mesozoic. Why should they suddenly turn into bitter enemies?

Any theory of the extinction, moreover, has to take into account the fact that it wasn't just the dinosaurs that died out. The pterosaurs and marine reptiles died out as well, along with almost 90 percent of the smallest sea-dwelling animals.

Even more remarkable was the number of creatures that survived. Small reptiles such as turtles, snakes, and lizards survived, along with the mammals and the birds. If some terrible disaster happened at the end of the Cretaceous, why weren't these animals killed as well?

Most theories of the extinction agree that there was probably a sudden change in the environment about 65 million years ago, a change that the dinosaurs and the other now-extinct animals did not survive. Perhaps the weather became different—colder, maybe, or warmer. Both possibilities have been suggested. If the temperature suddenly dropped, the dinosaurs might literally have died of the cold. This would be true whether they were cold-blooded or warm-blooded. If they were cold-blooded, they would have eventually lost the huge amount of heat that they kept stored in their large bodies. This might have taken a long time, but once a reptile the size of a dinosaur lost its body heat, it would have taken a long time to get it back. If the weather had turned colder, the animal might never have become warm again.

If the dinosaurs were warm-blooded, on the other hand, the cold would have killed them the same way it would have killed a naked mammal. A human being, trapped in the cold without clothing, would die within hours.

Dinosaurs had no furry coats to protect them from icy weather. The marine reptiles that died off all tended to live in shallow waters, not far from the shore. They would have been just as much affected by the change in climate as their land-dwelling relatives. The pterosaurs would also have had their lifestyles disrupted by this change in temperature. As the weather became colder, it would also have become more violent—windier and gustier. The pterosaurs were adapted for floating on gentle breezes. They could never have survived rough weather.

Notice also that only small reptiles lived through the extinction. These tiny creatures could have burrowed into the ground or found shelter in foliage until warm weather returned. Possibly this change in weather was seasonal rather than year round. The reptiles could have hibernated during the winter and come back out of hibernation during the summer.

The mammals, on the other hand, were furry and already tended to live in underground burrows. They were well adapted for harsher weather conditions.

What could have caused this sudden change in temperature? It might have been the result of a catastrophe in outer space.

One possibility is that a nearby star exploded. This would have sent dangerous radiation shooting through space, perhaps into the earth's atmosphere. This, in turn, would have caused chemical changes in the portion of the atmosphere called the ozone layer. These chemical changes would have allowed more light from the sun to reach the earth's surface.

Surprisingly, this would have actually lowered the temperature on earth rather than raising it. The hot rays of the sun would have caused the water near the surface of the ocean to evaporate—turn into water vapor—and form thicker clouds, which would then have shut out the sunlight. Temperatures would have dropped. Weather conditions would have become harsher. The radiation from the explosion of the star would also have been unhealthy for the dinosaurs themselves, thereby contributing to their demise more directly.

The problem with this exploding-star theory is that the extinctions would have happened very quickly, probably within a few years. And there is some evidence in the fossil record that the dinosaurs died out gradually, over a few million years.

There are other possible reasons for a drop in temperature, some of them more down to earth. We saw in the first chapter that the earth's continents are drifting, moving across the planet's surface like rafts on the ocean, although much more slowly. In the time of the dinosaurs, the continents were all clumped together on one side of the earth, with one great ocean surrounding them and another running right through the middle of the land. The continents themselves were filled with lakes and inland seas. This had an important effect on the weather and therefore on the dinosaurs, who, because of the configuration of the land, were never very far from water.

Water has a way of retaining heat. During the summer, for instance, a body of water will collect heat slowly, for months on end. This is why the water at the beach is always colder in June than it is in August. It just hasn't had time to warm up yet.

On the other hand, once the water becomes warm it can stay warm for a long time, releasing its heat slowly.

Consider what this means. Throughout the Mesozoic, the continents were covered with inland lakes and seas. During the summer, these bodies of water would have absorbed a great deal of heat, keeping the air cool. During the winter, on the other hand, they would have slowly released the heat that they had collected over the summer, keeping the air warm. Therefore, the air temperatures in winter wouldn't have been that much different from the air temperatures in the summer.

As the continents drifted apart, however, the inland seas would have begun to dry up. The water vanished. Winters would have become much colder than summers. Only those animals that were adapted for cold winters—the mammals, birds, and small reptiles—would have survived.

All of this is pure guesswork, however. Nobody is even sure if temperatures became colder at the end of the Cretaceous. Maybe they became warmer, in which case the dinosaurs may well have died from heat prostration.

The most dramatic theory yet offered for the death of the dinosaurs, however, is that the earth collided with an asteroid.

Asteroids are large chunks of rock that orbit the sun in much the same way as the earth does. Most of them are found between the orbits of Mars and Jupiter, but there are a few that actually pass fairly close to the earth. It has been estimated that the earth collides with one of these asteroids once every 100 million years or so. There are some very large craters on earth that are apparently a result of these collisions—Meteor Crater in Winslow, Arizona, for instance.

Such a collision would be a genuine catastrophe; some of the asteroids are several miles wide. If one had landed in the ocean at the end of the Cretaceous (which would explain why we haven't been able to find a crater from this period), it would have thrown large amounts of debris into the upper atmosphere. This debris would have formed clouds so thick that the sunlight would have been almost entirely cut off. Day would have turned into night. Plants and sea creatures that depended on the sun for their survival would have died. Then the animals that ate these plants and animals would have died. Then the animals that ate the animals that ate the plants and animals would have died. And so on. Only the smaller animals, ones that needed relatively little food, would have lived through the long night.

There is actually some evidence that this may have happened. A few years ago scientists were examining rocks formed during the Cretaceous era. There was an element in the rock samples called iridium. Iridium is a very heavy element. For this reason, most of the iridium on earth sank to the center of our planet long ago. The only iridium on the earth's surface comes from outer space, in meteorites.

The presence of iridium in the Cretaceous rock samples was not unusual. What was unusual was that the amount of iridium suddenly went up 8,000 percent at the very end of the Cretaceous. This means that a large amount of the element must have arrived abruptly from outer space. Could it have arrived on an asteroid?

That seems possible. Scientists, however, have many different opinions on this subject.

There are any number of theories as to what happened to the dinosaurs. The ones discussed so far in this chapter barely scratch the surface. Possibly, the real reason for the Great Cretaceous Extinction is a combination of several of these theories. Or maybe we haven't hit on the real reason yet.

Whatever it was that killed the dinosaurs, though, there's no question that it was very successful. All the dinosaurs are quite dead.

Or are they?

Meteor Crater near Winslow, Arizona.
Could a hit by a meteorite or asteroid have
caused the disappearance of the dinosaurs?

Archaeopteryx, once thought to be a bird,
might really have been a dinosaur.
Does this mean that birds are the living
descendants of the once-mighty dinosaurs?

Is it possible that, if you looked out your window right now, you might see a dinosaur perched on the limb of a tree across the street? Or did you perhaps have roast dinosaur for dinner last Thanksgiving?

Are birds dinosaurs?

More than a few well-known paleontologists would say that birds are indeed dinosaurs. The only real difference is that they are warm-blooded and have feathers.

As we saw earlier, the dinosaurs may have been warm-blooded. And some may have had feathers as well.

In 1877, a fossil skeleton was unearthed in Bavaria. At first, its discoverers believed it to be a dinosaur skeleton. Then they noticed that the rock around the skeleton contained a clear impression of feathers. The skeleton, they decided, must have belonged to a bird. They named it *Archaeopteryx* ("ancient wing").

Until just a few years ago, *Archaeopteryx* was regarded as the oldest bird known. All at once, though, paleontologists have come to suspect that *Archaeopteryx* was not a bird at all. It may have been a dinosaur, specifically, a kind of coelurosaur, one of the early dinosaurs that we studied in Chapter Four. Almost certainly it was unable to fly. Probably the feathers were there to keep it warm, although they may have helped it to leap into the air on occasion.

When *Archaeopteryx* was believed to have been a bird, it was thought that it was a cousin of the dinosaurs, probably descended from the thecodonts. Now that *Archaeopteryx* is suspected to have been a dinosaur, that picture has changed considerably. *Archaeopteryx*, or its immediate relatives, may be the direct ancestor of the birds. This means that birds can be considered a kind of dinosaur, and this opens up a whole new picture of life in the Mesozoic.

Dinosaurs on the whole were probably a great deal more birdlike than we ever imagined. They may have moved like birds, looked a little like birds, and behaved like birds.

They didn't survive like birds, though. When the Cretaceous ended and the other dinosaurs died, the birds went right on living. They're still with us today. Along with the crocodiles, they are the last legacy of the archosaurs and possibly the last surviving dinosaurs.

Which means that the dinosaur story may have had a happy ending after all.

Epilog

The dinosaur is a very misunderstood animal. The term *dinosaur* has become a kind of insult. If you call something a "dinosaur," you mean that it is large and obsolete, that it doesn't fit in. In other words, you mean something that isn't too successful at filling its ecological niche.

Yet this isn't what the dinosaurs were like at all. They were extremely successful. They spread over the entire earth. There were dinosaurs on every continent. They dominated this planet for more than 135 million years. The mammals, in their turn, have been in charge for only about 60 million. Human beings have been around for only 3 million. We should do as well as the dinosaurs. There are some people who are afraid that we won't.

The human race seems to fill its ecological niche better than any other species in history. Yet it may be in danger of filling it too well. Humans are the most advanced predators that the world has ever seen, more terrifying in our own world than *Tyrannosaurus rex* was in its. There is little chance that we will ever be dominated by any other species, as long as we have our large brains and our advanced technology.

And as long as we don't destroy our own ecological niche.

The Great Cretaceous Extinction was only one of several moments in history when a large number of species disappeared from the face of the earth all at once. There was another at the end of the Paleozoic, and a smaller one at the end of the Triassic. And there will probably be another at the end of the Cenozoic. In fact, we may be going through the Great Cenozoic Extinction right now.

Over the last 30,000 years or so, animals have become extinct at an alarming rate. In recent years, the extinctions seem to be coming faster than ever. This time, however, we don't have to theorize about what is causing the extinctions. We know what's causing them. Human beings are causing them.

Ever since the first hunting societies developed, thousands of years ago, human beings have killed animals by the millions—for food, game, and sport. Human beings are hunters, almost certainly the greatest hunters that have yet evolved. But if we get any better, there won't be anything left to hunt. And then where will we be?

The Cenozoic will be over. Human beings will almost certainly go the way of the dinosaur. But unlike the dinosaurs, we won't be extinguished by natural forces. We will have committed suicide.

We do have a choice in the matter. The Great Cenozoic Extinction does not have to take place. Not right away, anyway. If human beings learn to live within their ecological niche, rather than destroy it, we can establish a place for ourselves as the most successful animals ever to evolve on this planet. We can live as long as the dinosaurs, or even longer.

Or we can bring the age of mammals to an abrupt finish. It's up to us. It's up to you.

Glossary

Amphibian—an animal that can live both in and out of water, but that must remain near water in order to reproduce. Amphibians are the evolutionary link between fish and reptiles. Frogs and salamanders are examples of modern amphibians.

Ankylosaurs—armored dinosaurs; one of the five major types of ornithiscian dinosaur.*

Archosaurs—the subclass of reptiles to which the dinosaurs belong. Other types of archosaurs are the crocodilians, the pterosaurs, and the thecodonts. Only the crocodilians have survived to the present day, although some authorities argue that birds, which may be direct descendants of dinosaurs, should be considered a type of archosaur.

*Specific dinosaur names are not included in this glossary. See the Index for page references to them.

Atoms—the basic building blocks of which all material things, including living organisms, are made.

Carnivorous—meat-eating; refers to animals that eat the flesh of other animals. The theropods were carnivorous.

Cenozoic—one of the seven eras of paleontological time; the age of "new life." We are still in the Cenozoic today. Sometimes the Cenozoic is referred to as the "age of mammals" because during this era mammals became the dominant animals.

Ceratopsians—armored dinosaurs; one of the five major types of ornithischian dinosaur.

Cold-blooded—lacking internal temperature controls; refers to animals with internal temperatures that vary according to the external temperature. All (or most, according to some theories) reptiles are cold-blooded.

Cretaceous—the last of the three divisions of the Mesozoic era.

Crocodilians—one of the five kinds of archosaurs, the only one still surviving today.

Dinosaur—popular term for two types of archosaurs, the ornithischians and the saurischians.

Ecological niche—the particular way in which a species of living organism survives within its particular environment.

Evolution—the tendency of living creatures to change over time, usually in response to their environment.

Extinction—the disappearance of a species of living organism.

Fossils—the remains of animals that lived in past ages.

Hadrosaurs—duck-billed dinosaurs; one of the five major types of ornithischian dinosaur, often distinguished by a bizarre crest on the top of the skull.

Herbivorous—plant-eating; refers to animals that eat only vegetation and not other animals. Most dinosaurs, with the exception of the theropods, were herbivorous.

Jurassic—the second of the three divisions of the Mesozoic era.

Lungfish—a type of fish that can survive out of water for a limited time; lungfish were probably the ancestors of the amphibians.

Mammals—a type of animal distinguished by hair, warm-bloodedness, mammary glands (from which they get their name), and the birth of live young. Humans are mammals, as are most large, land-dwelling animals today.

Mesozoic—one of the seven major divisions of geologic time; the age of "middle life." Sometimes referred to as the age of reptiles, because reptiles (especially dinosaurs) dominated the earth during this era.

Molecules—chains of atoms. All living organisms are made up of molecules.

Mutation—a change in a living organism that can be passed on from generation to generation.

Natural selection—the tendency of certain animals to survive in their ecological niches better than other animals. Together with mutation, natural selection is the driving force behind evolution.

Paleontology—the study of organisms that lived on earth in past ages.

Paleozoic—one of the eight major divisions of geologic time; the age of "old life." The reptiles evolved near the end of the Paleozoic era.

Permian—the last period of the Paleozoic era.

Pterosaurs—flying reptiles.

Radiative evolution—a form of evolution in which new species evolve very quickly to fill a large number of newly available ecological niches.

Reptiles—a type of animal distinguished by cold-bloodedness and scaly skin.

Saurischians—one of the two types of dinosaurs, distinguished by hips resembling those of lizards (as opposed to the ornithischians, which had hips resembling those of birds).

Sauropods—one of the major types of saurischian dinosaur. The sauropods were herbivorous and generally very large.

Thecodonts—early Triassic reptiles, first of the archosaurs and ancestors of the dinosaurs.

Therapsids—late Permian reptiles, ancestors of the modern mammal. Sometimes called the "mammal-like reptiles."

Theropods—one of the two major types of saurischian dinosaur. Theropods were the only carnivorous dinosaurs and are therefore sometimes referred to as the carnosaurs.

Triassic—the first of the three periods of the Mesozoic era.

Warm-blooded—having internal temperature controls; refers to living organisms that maintain the same internal temperature no matter what the external temperature (unless external temperatures become extreme). All mammals are warm-blooded.

Suggested Reading

Asimov, Isaac. *How Did We Find Out About Dinosaurs?* New York: Walker & Co., n.d.

Cohen, Daniel. *What Really Happened to the Dinosaurs?* New York: Dutton, 1977.

Colbert, Edwin H. *Dinosaur World.* Straven; 1977.

____________. *The Year of the Dinosaur.* New York: Scribners, 1977.

Desmond, Adrian. *The Hot-Blooded Dinosaurs: A Revolution in Paleontology.* New York: Dial Press, 1976.

Halstead, Beverly. *A Closer Look at Prehistoric Reptiles.* London: Franklin Watts, 1978.

Jabor, William. *Whatever Happened to the Dinosaurs?* New York: Julian Messner, 1978.

Lambert, David. *Exploring the Age of Dinosaurs.* London: Franklin Watts, 1978.

Matthews, William H., III. *Wonders of the Dinosaur World.* New York: Dodd, Mead, 1963.

Ostrom, John H. *The Strange World of Dinosaurs.* New York: Putnam, 1969.

Rosenbloom, Joseph. *Dictionary of Dinosaurs.* New York: Julian Messner, 1980.

Index